REAL ESTATE
INSIGHTS
VOLUME 2

REAL ESTATE
INSIGHTS
V O L U M E 2

Conversations With Leading
Real Estate Professionals

AMERICA'S LEADING REAL
ESTATE PROFESSIONALS

FEATURING:

Chelsey Franklin

Don Prigge

Jeff Gordon

Kevin McGrath

Melissa Vance

Erin Newman

Tammy Potter

Real Estate Insights Volume 2/ Mark Imperial —1ˢᵗ ed.
Managing Editor/ Shannon Buritz

ISBN-13: 978-1-954757-01-1

Remarkable Press™

Royalties from the retail sales of **"REAL ESTATE INSIGHTS Volume 2: CONVERSATIONS WITH AMERICA'S LEADING REAL ESTATE PROFESSIONALS"** are donated to the Global Autism Project:

AUTISM KNOWS NO BORDERS;
FORTUNATELY NEITHER DO WE.®

The Global Autism Project 501(C)3 is a nonprofit organization that provides training to local individuals in evidence-based practice for individuals with autism.

The Global Autism Project believes that every child has the ability to learn, and their potential should not be limited by geographical bounds.

The Global Autism Project seeks to eliminate the disparity in service provision seen around the world by providing high-quality training to individuals providing services in their local community. This training is made sustainable through regular training trips and contiguous remote training.

You can learn more about the Global Autism Project by visiting **GlobalAutismProject.org.**

CONTENTS

A NOTE TO THE READER

Thank you for buying your copy of "REAL ESTATE INSIGHTS Volume 2: Conversations With America's Leading Real Estate Professionals." This book was originally created as a series of live interviews; that's why it reads like a series of conversations, rather than a traditional book that talks at you.

I wanted you to feel as though the participants and I are talking with you, much like a close friend or relative, and felt that creating the material this way would make it easier for you to grasp the topics and put them to use quickly, rather than wading through hundreds of pages.

So relax, grab a pen and paper, take notes, and get ready to learn some fascinating Real Estate Insights.

Warmest regards,

Mark Imperial

Publisher, Author, and Radio Personality

INTRODUCTION

"REAL ESTATE INSIGHTS Volume 2: Conversations With America's Leading Real Estate Professionals" is a collaborative book series featuring leading Real Estate Professionals from across the country.

Remarkable Press™ would like to extend a heartfelt thank you to all participants who took the time to submit their chapter and offer their support in becoming ambassadors for this project.

100% of the royalties from this book's retail sales will be donated to the Global Autism Project. Should you want to make a direct donation, visit their website at GlobalAutismProject.org

Conversation with Chelsey Franklin

Tell us about your business and the people you specialize in helping.

Chelsey Franklin: We represent buyers and sellers across the Denver Metro and primarily Northern Colorado. I have a team of three licensed agents and a full-time transaction coordinator. We will sell around $40 million in 2020. So that's our bread and butter.

How has the pandemic affected the Denver real estate market?

Chelsey Franklin: Everyone was speculating in early 2020 that there would be some sort of shift happening. It hasn't been related to real estate at all. As we know, interest rates are historically low. Denver just doesn't have the inventory. Colorado is one of the top five fastest-growing states. We have many people moving here, especially with COVID, more people can work from home than ever before. With that being said, nothing has slowed down for us. Last month we had record sales for our team, closing on 17 homes. Next month is projected to do the same. There are lots of bidding wars, and it is very much a seller's market right now.

What makes Colorado such an attractive place to buy a home?

Chelsey Franklin: Denver is right smack dab in the middle of things that draw people to Colorado, such as outdoor lifestyle, tons of hiking, skiing, and mountain activities. It's a beautiful state and a beautiful place to be. Many tourists come out, and they just never leave.

What is your number one piece of advice for people coming in from out of town and interested in the Denver area?

Chelsey Franklin: Most of our marketing aims to capture people moving into the area and become their local experts. There are so many excellent suburbs. It's not just Denver Metro. There are various great neighborhoods, and we can help you decide which one would be the best fit. If you're on the east side towards Stapleton, it provides more city life. If you want suburban areas, we can direct you to Metro districts with great schools. Downtown Denver offers high rise lifestyles. Based on your interests, we will guide you in the right direction.

What are the most popular states that people are migrating to you from?

Chelsey Franklin: We have many California transplants. Also, Texas, Chicago, and Florida. Those are the big ones.

What inspired you to get into real estate?

Chelsey Franklin: I played collegiate golf at the University of Oklahoma. I have my Master's in Intercollegiate Athletic Administration. So I felt pigeonholed to just coach or do something higher education-related. I wanted to have a family, and my husband went to law school, so my dad suggested getting into real estate. It just kind of took off from there. Since I believe in "practicing what you preach," we put all of our extra money into the ground, into real estate. I think everyone needs to own as much dirt as possible. After all, it's the only thing we are going to run out of eventually. We have about 35 rental properties and are still growing.

I will say that flipping houses has been the most challenging aspect of the pandemic. Since Colorado is low on inventory, it can be challenging to find a home to flip. We aim for around six projects a year, but most first time homebuyers are snatching up those properties, which isn't a bad thing because we also would be more than happy to broker a deal for you on the same home. And if I can't sell it, I'll flip it.

Is working with investors another specialty of yours?

Chelsey Franklin: Yes, it is. I can help them run numbers, run them quickly, and calculate our rates of return. I've got a lot of great lenders, wholesalers, and contractors. Knowing your numbers and knowing what to expect when you are buying something is essential. From my own experience, I can tell people what to look at and what to steer clear of. This ends up being a perk for many of my clients.

If people would like to work with you and benefit from your expertise, how can they connect with you?

Chelsey Franklin: My mantra for 2020 has just been to work with friendly people. We will help you buy and sell anything. We've sold everything from mobile homes to two million dollar estates this year, and we love helping with all of that and everything in between. If you are looking to buy, sell, invest, or build, we have someone on our team specializing in it. Let us know what your needs are. Our website is shopcoloradohouses.com, and you can always reach me on my cell at 720-232-8796.

CHELSEY FRANKLIN

Real Estate Broker and Investor
Team Lead, Franklin Team at RE/MAX Alliance

Hi! I am the team lead for the Franklin Team. My team and I absolutely love helping our clients achieve their goals. We take pride in our ability to make each client feel valued and informed throughout the entire transaction. We know what it takes to be successful and efficiently market our listings, so they receive maximum exposure; and, for our buyers, we effectively utilize both front range MLS systems and other resources to maximize the potential of finding their dream property for the best price possible.

I have three kids: Bailey Lynn, Maddie Rae, and James Harvey. My husband is a named partner at Cowan, Hubbert, & Franklin. In our free time, the Franklin's enjoy all things Colorado, including golfing (Brooke and I are both former D1 athletes and 4-time letter winners at the University of Oklahoma), skiing, hiking, and long walks with our dog followed by a glass of wine or whiskey! We look forward to the opportunity of working with you!

WEBSITE:

shopcoloradohouses.com

EMAIL:

chelsey@shopcoloradohouses.com

PHONE:

720-232-8796

FACEBOOK:

https://www.facebook.com/franklinteamRE

LINKEDIN:

https://www.linkedin.com/in/chelsey-franklin-a1a69361/

Conversation with Donald M. Prigge

Tell us about your business and the people you specialize in helping.

Donald M. Prigge: I'm a managing broker. Therefore, I don't sell, but I have 55 people I oversee and help sell. We sell everything, including residential, commercial, and industrial. I have agents in the office that do all of it. Our bread and butter are primarily residential. The company is Baird and Warner, and we've been in business for 165 years. Though we are

America's oldest real estate company, I believe we are also the most progressive.

How has the pandemic affected your real estate market? What changes have you seen?

Donald M. Prigge: From a real estate standpoint, everything and nothing has changed. Real estate companies and agents are a little slow on the uptake when it comes to changes. We had to learn in five weeks what we would have probably learned in five years. So it changed a lot. And yet it changes nothing because there are still buyers buying houses and sellers selling houses. But I think it changes the way we go about it. We do a lot more virtual now than ever before. There are virtual tours, virtual open houses, and we've even sold homes where the buyer doesn't see it in person until the final walkthrough. A lot of that isn't necessarily new because we have been doing virtual for some time with transferees. But across the board, it certainly changed beginning in March 2020. There has been some pivoting, and we had to change dramatically to find ways to get the average buyer accustomed to virtual.

What are the biggest concerns of buyers and sellers today?

Donald M. Prigge: The most significant concerns have been safety related across the board. I have been doing this for 46 years, and it has always been done the same way. The buyers will get in my car, I will drive them around to houses, and we will have a good time. Now all of a sudden, this is a concern. Getting in someone else's car is currently somewhat of an antiquated way of doing business. We now meet at the house, glove up, mask up, and complete the tour.

We advise sellers to pre-clean and also clean when we are done.

In addition to safety issues, due to a strong seller's market with escalating prices, multiple offers, and a shortage of inventories, sellers are concerned that they will sell their home quickly and not find a home to purchase. This potential issue can generally be handled by partnering with a professional in real estate to provide guidance and options to the sellers.

Are you finding that people's priorities or reasons for moving have changed?

Donald M. Prigge: Absolutely. One of the most recent changes is that homes are now becoming classrooms and office spaces. The needs of the house and the housing function has changed. A lot of houses are not proving to be adequate for what this new life consists of. Many people are also looking for larger yards or pools since they can't go out. Mansions are back since people need more space. Second homes are becoming important because that is where families are taking their vacations. Luxury home sales and lake property sales are on the rise as well. Though the reasons have changed, the need is still there. People are just looking differently at how they are going to use the house.

What inspired you to get started in real estate?

Donald M. Prigge: The long story short is that I received a knock on my door from my landlord in 1974. I was living in a two-flat at the time with one upper and one lower unit. He asked me if I wanted to buy the building. After the laughter stopped, I said, "How is that going to happen? I am having a hard time paying my rent." He then explained to me the process of collecting the rent from the upstairs tenant and not making a payment. He worked out a deal with me called an installment contract for warranty deed. Essentially, this means I used his money (since I had none), and I bought the house for a couple of thousand dollars down. I collected the rent upstairs, had no payment, and started my buying spree based on that. I realized how lucrative it was after I bought three or four houses on the street. I thought it was such a great idea that I started knocking on doors and saying to people, "When you are ready to sell, call me. I'll buy it." All of a sudden, I had a new career. I just kind of stumbled into it. In the last 46 years, I have worked every aspect of real estate. I did rehab before HGTV thought of it. I have flipped shopping centers and hotels. So I've been around for a long time. It has been lucrative, so I guess I'll stick with it.

How can people who could benefit from your expertise find you and connect with you?

Donald M. Prigge: Feel free to text me at 847-915-5095. You can also email me at don.prigge@baird-warner.com.

DONALD M. PRIGGE, REALTOR EMERITUS

Designated Managing Broker
Baird and Warner Real Estate

Donald M. Prigge literally fell into real estate. As a lineman for the electric company from 18 to 24, Donald was 6'6", clumsy and uncoordinated. He fell off of two poles! His crew leader said to him, "You are not very good at this, are you?" He then explained that he owned a two-person real estate company. Donald made it a three-person company. This happened right about the time his landlord convinced him to buy his first two-unit building. Donald bought his first investment property the following year with no money down... precisely what he had! He flipped it for a 50% increase in 90 days. In the next 45+ years in real estate, Donald has sold all types of real estate, managed offices, owned offices, trained thousands of real estate brokers, owned a new construction company, rehabbed, flipped houses to hotels, repurposed restaurants, and done an uncountable amount of seminars and convention addresses throughout America. He had many successes and a few "learning" lessons along the way. Donald has five children (two girls, three boys) and a beautiful wife. Life is good!

WEBSITE:

donaldprigge.bairdwarner.com

EMAIL:

Themarv@att.net

LINKEDIN:

linkedin.com/in/donald-prigge-6528565

FACEBOOK:

Facebook.com/don.prigge

TWITTER:

DonPrigge@BairdWarnerMgr

OFFICE:

815-788-2100

FAX:

847-915-5095

Conversation with Jeff Gordon

Tell us about your particular business and the people you specialize in helping.

Jeff Gordon: We are a full-service organization specializing in the sale & lease of residential and light commercial real estate and investment properties in Massachusetts and New Hampshire. There isn't any big box, heavy or industrial commercial real estate to deal with around my area. EXIT Assurance Realty (EXITassurance.com) has been in business for 18+

years in Groton, MA. We are very well known in the area, and proudly, we have a terrific reputation.

How has the recent pandemic affected the real estate market in your area?

Jeff Gordon: No effect at all. As a matter of fact, we've been busier than ever. Our sales are way up. It's all a function of the interest rates that are in play from the Fed. I'll give you an example. We are in a fierce seller's market right now. Currently, from the standpoint of single-family homes in Groton, there are eight active listings. In the past six months, 81 have sold. That is a massive seller's market. We're seeing over asking price on almost every deal. Money is being spent everywhere, from additions to driveways, to rock walls, to decks. Money is coming out of the woodwork, especially when there's a gap between a bank's appraised value and the asking price of the sale. Buyers are paying $10,000, $20,000, $30,000, or $50,000 over the asking price and bridging the gap between the appraised value and the selling price. It's amazing and scary at the same time. Since the mortgage market crash, we could depend on the appraisers to keep values in check. Home values were tempered, kept from escalating too much and too fast. I'm not sure that's the case now.

Around the country, many people were worried about the real estate markets, and obviously, they're affected in different ways. What would you say is the difference in your area? Are people's priorities changing?

Jeff Gordon: I am not seeing priorities being any different than what they were before COVID. The mortgage rates are definitely spawning the buyers, whether it be refinancing or purchases. I can't point to any recent buyer circumstance that caused them to relocate from the city of Boston, Worcester, or elsewhere, specifically because of COVID. The typical reasons for a purchase or sale are consistent; job change, upsize, downsize, school system selection, etc. The Groton Dunstable Regional School District is exceptional and rated one of the best in Massachusetts. Of course, we have two private High Schools here too; the Groton School and Lawrence Academy! There's going to be huge momentum in real estate sales in the coming years with the completion of the Indian Hill Music Center. It's going to put Groton, MA on the map as a desirable destination location, much like Lenox, MA, where Tanglewood is located. It's a big deal! And together with the other attractions this area has to offer, like the lakes & streams, rivers, walking trails, conservation areas, farming, education, and now professional music, Groton will be a very desirable area.

REAL ESTATE INSIGHTS VOLUME 2

What precautions are being taken now? Do more people want to do virtual walkthroughs?

Jeff Gordon: We're seeing just as many people as we did before, if not more. We have more precautions in place and use face masks, hand sanitizers, and gloves during walkthroughs. Some sellers don't want people walking through the property with shoes on. I have also been offering people Clorox wipes at the door and having them wipe down anything they touch. It hasn't been difficult at all to implement these new safety practices.

What inspired you to get started in real estate?

Jeff Gordon: I was in Enterprise Software sales for 18 years. My most recent venture was a startup. And long story short, it ceased operations. It really tainted me down, and I decided I didn't want to go back to the industry. I remembered a friend of mine, Mark Bettinson, the Broker/Owner of EXIT Premier Real Estate in Burlington, MA. He invited me to come down and talk about a career in real estate. It took me 20 seconds to understand EXIT's business model and compensation model, and I decided that's what I was going to do. I literally bought the EXIT franchise and got my sales agency license in the same week. I completely changed careers. EXIT Assurance Realty was born, and my first listing was a $1.4 million home in Carlisle, MA!

Is there anything else you would like to share?

Jeff Gordon: For a while now, I've wanted to coach potential buyers and sellers on how they should qualify an agent. And that is through testimonials. Consumers often make the mistake of just looking at Zillow, Realtor.com, or even Google reviews. But the real place to go and research a real estate agent is their actual website! For years now, I have been posting testimonials to my own website. EXIT Assurance Realty has so many testimonials that people don't see unless they visit our homepage. You can better understand the agent's work and reputation from a particular agent's website. DON'T depend on sheerly the number of reviews an agent has on Zillow, for example, because they can be posted under false pretenses.

The second piece of advice is to work with a Realtor® instead of just a real estate agent. There's a big difference, believe me. Realtor's abide by a higher level of education, discipline, and ethics. All of our sales professionals are Realtors. Not negotiable.

For people in your area thinking about buying or selling, how can they get in contact with you?

Jeff Gordon: I'm located in Groton, Massachusetts, and we service all of Massachusetts and Southern New Hampshire. I'm a licensed Broker in both states. We have 14 agents in our company with great personalities. They're well-trained, knowledgeable, and genuinely care about their clients. I can be reached at 508-864-7487. You can also download my electronic business card by going to the website JeffGordon.pro.

JEFF GORDON

———◦———

MA and NH Broker/Owner, EXIT Assurance Realty

Jeff started his real estate career 18 years ago, after a diverse work history in direct sales management. He worked for 19 years with several startup software companies in the manufacturing, design and supply chain management space.

In late 2001, after much encouragement from his father-in-law to become an entrepreneur, Jeff purchased an EXIT Realty franchise and earned his Sales Agent's license in the same week! EXIT Assurance Realty in Groton, MA, was born.

Jeff is the Broker/Owner of EXIT Assurance Realty, and his Real Estate Brokerage has helped thousands of people buy and/or sell real estate, and securely transition their future.

As Broker/Owner, Jeff's passion is to build great Sales Agents. He says, "Good Agents are born. Great Agents are trained." Included in his training regimen are core values. Jeff's core values are focused

on "being there and being present. Not the money."
That's how we roll.

Professionally, Jeff is a licensed Broker in Massachusetts and New Hampshire. He has earned his C2EX designation, a nationally recognized achievement for Professional Real Estate Services, and is also a Certified Negotiation Expert.

On a personal note, Jeff plays ice hockey, fishes, and likes to spend time with friends, family, children, and grandchildren. He is the President of the Groton Business Association, and a Board Member of the Prescott School Community Center in Groton, MA.

WEBSITE:

jeffgordon.EXITassurance.com

EMAIL:

jeff@EXITassurance.com

LINKEDIN:

https://www.linkedin.com/in/jeff-gordon-4213171/

FACEBOOK:

https://www.facebook.com/MYEXIT

TWITTER:

https://twitter.com/GrotonRealtor

OFFICE:

978-448-6800

CELL:

508-864-7487

BLOG:

https://www.jeffgordon.exitassurance.com/blogs/

Conversation with Kevin McGrath

Tell us about your business and the people you specialize in helping.

Kevin McGrath: I am the managing broker of the Long & Foster real estate office in Fredericksburg, Virginia; we have about 100 agents. In addition to doing some listing and selling, I spend most of my time recruiting new agents, helping new agents succeed, and developing training programs.

How has the current pandemic affected the real estate market in your area?

Kevin McGrath: Well, that's an interesting question. What I always fall back to is that all real estate is local. What we see in Fredericksburg is probably vastly different from what is happening in rural Pennsylvania or Iowa. Our monthly sales have consistently exceeded the same months from last year. We have a real lack of inventory, often seeing days on the market as low as six, multiple offers are the norm, and we still have historically low-interest rates. That being said, we still had to shift gears in how we market properties and set up homes for showing.

Are the priorities of your clients different now than they were pre-pandemic?

Kevin McGrath: From a buyer's perspective, they are often worn out and discouraged after losing out on two or three properties and want to know how to win the next bidding war. The sellers are concerned with how they can show their property and still keep their family safe. We put several things into place, including notices around the property related to COVID-19, hand sanitizer, booties, etc. It is essential to explain to the seller exactly how the showings are going to work. People get upset when the unexpected happens, so you have to take that out of the equation. Let them know, "Hey, we are going to get this house sold, and here's how we are going to do it safely."

What is the number one piece of advice for buyers and sellers in today's market that is more important than ever?

Kevin McGrath: This is a tough thing to explain to buyers without sounding like a pushy salesman, but the house you want to think about and "sleep on" is the same house someone is putting an offer on right now. Also, the listing price is a starting point now. On average, a home will go on the market for $400,000 and will sell for $425,000. If you come in under list, you aren't even in the game. The market moves very quickly. I teach real estate classes at the local Realtor Association, and I always say that real estate moves in hours and minutes, not days and weeks. You need to let your clients know how quickly things are moving today and what they need to do to keep up, and it's vital to create and share your expectations on timely communication.

What inspired you to get started in real estate?

Kevin McGrath: I always wanted to do it. I was in the building supply industry for 20 years. We all remember what happened in 2005, and that industry took a hit. I told myself I was either going to do it now or never do it. I started working at an excellent local brokerage called Coldwell Banker Elite. Things were tough & I started thinking I might have to go get a "real job." Then one day, I answered the phone, and it was a bank in California, and she said, "We need an agent to help us with a foreclosed property." I had no idea what she was talking about. I thought it was a prank call, but I had nothing going on, so I went through the process, and she said, "Great, can you take five more properties?" I accepted, even though I had to Google BPO because I had no idea what that meant (Broker's Price Opinion), which is sort of like an appraisal. Fast forward a little, and in 2008 I sold 210 homes, and the moral of the story is that you can always find ways to do good business in bad times. Through the success there, I joined up with a partner, Jane Wallace, and we opened our own RE/MAX brokerage. We had that for five years and were very successful. Long & Foster acquired my company at the end of that term, and I ended up coming to work here, and the experience has been excellent.

How can buyers and sellers in your area find you and connect with you?

Kevin McGrath: My email address is fredva@LNF. com. You can also find us at longandfoster.com. My cell phone number is 540-604-1843. I am a hands-on agent, a hands-on manager, and I am always available to assist anyone with their particular needs. We have 100 highly trained agents and are one of the largest brokerages in the area. We handle everything from mortgages to titles to insurance to sales.

KEVIN MCGRATH

———————✦———————

Managing Broker, Long & Foster Real Estate

All it took was one phone call and a little bit of luck. I was whiling away another endless afternoon manning the front desk at the local brokerage here in good ol' Fredericksburg, supposedly in an effort to snare potential home buyers, as if one would ever really walk through the door, but really not doing much more than hoping a red three was somewhere in the deck, and that it would magically appear before time ran out. I had all but given up, and 5 o'clock had come and gone, so I start packing my computer and all other stuff that is supposed to make me look like a real Realtor, hoping to make good my escape quickly and quietly.

And then the phone rang. Thinking optimistically that I had nothing to lose, I snatched the receiver to my ear, quickly belting out my best real estate greeting, hoping they would ask a question that I could sort of fake my way out of with some sort of answer so they would not be able to read how green I was, and that the ink on my license was barely dry. Right away, I can feel that I'm only half-listening as she starts to tell me she is calling from a "bank" in California. Already mentally hanging up, I quickly pause as she says, "We have a property in Fredericksburg we need an agent to check on." Again, going back to that whole thinking optimistically thing from the beginning of the paragraph, I took down the address and agreed to go by there and take a look.

It turned out to be only a few miles from the office, and the young man who answered the door seemed a little "confused." Since I really had no idea what to ask him, much less any real idea of what I was doing there, it was a pretty short conversation, so I headed home and didn't give it much thought.

The next morning I sent an email to the bank letting them know that the property was occupied and then went on about my day, which pretty much meant I got up and poured another cup of coffee.

I returned to my assigned workspace to find, believe it or not, a response from the bank advising me to offer Cash For Keys to the occupant, assist them in finding a new place to live, if necessary, and prepare the home for marketing as soon as possible. A listing agreement was also attached, which certainly lent a little credibility to a process that was starting to make me feel like I was trying to figure out what the number nine smelled like.

It was 2007, and I had just entered the world of Real Estate Foreclosures; and in the next 18 months, I sold over 200 homes.

Now, I can already hear you; who is this guy, and why is he bragging about how great he is? I'm not bragging. Well, not much anyway. My point is that when you sell 200+ homes in that amount of time, you get smart real fast, mostly out of necessity and repetition. I saw many contracts in those 18 months, probably over 400, and when you review that many contracts, some of it is bound to sink in.

So when you are shopping for your new home or selling your existing one, drop me a line. I've been around the block, I pretty much know the ins and outs of the home buying and selling process, and I'm confident that you will benefit from my experience.

EMAIL:

fredva@LNF.com

WEBSITE:

fredva.com

LINKEDIN:

linkedin.com/in/kevinmcgrathrealtor/

FACEBOOK:

facebook.com/FredericksburgRealtorVirginia

AMERICA'S LEADING REAL ESTATE PROFESSIONALS

TWITTER:

twitter.com/fredvarealty

OFFICE:

540-371-5220

CELL:

540-604-1843

FAX:

It's the 21st Century; I do not have a time machine...

Conversation with Melissa Vance

Tell us about your business and the people you specialize in helping.

Melissa Vance: I am currently in Manhattan, and this area has been going through a very interesting time post COVID since we were completely locked down. We weren't able to have showings until June 22. We started 2020 very, very strong, and then we went into complete lockdown in March. In the late summer, the market began to come back to life. What we're experiencing right now is a very active buyer's market. So if you ever thought of buying in New York, this is the time to do it because we have a lot of inventory. Usually, we have about 7,500 units listed. Compared to the 9,300 units listed that we have now - that's a 22% increase in inventory. Contracts are being signed, and the market has started to really move forward. Properties that are under a million dollars make up the majority of sales right now, which are about 48% of the market. Homes in the one million to two million dollar range make up 27%. That gives you a good idea of the average buyer in New York. We are seeing the most price negotiating in the more than $5 million market. If you find yourself in that particular price bracket, negotiability is at an all-time high.

> **In many other areas of the country, it is a seller's market with a really low inventory. Can you give us some insight into what is causing the opposite to happen in New York City?**

Melissa Vance: In New York, it's all about lifestyle. Restaurants in New York City opened indoor dining with a 25% capacity on September 30th. Broadway isn't opening until May of 2021. Unfortunately, office workers haven't come back to the office. Around 10% of the workforce is back in the office. People are not coming back into the city right now for multiple reasons. Also, there has been a disconnect about when schools were going to open in New York City. Parents are trying to adjust to half virtual and half in-school learning schedules for their children. At the beginning of the pandemic, many people went out to their vacation homes and stayed for the summer and now for the school year. There has also been an exodus of families with small children who have moved to New York City suburbs. They were probably planning to leave in two years or so, but the pandemic just moved their timeline up.

Now that there is an opportunity for buyers out there, what is the best advice you can give that is more important now than ever?

Melissa Vance: This is a great time to be buying in New York City. You definitely have a choice of neighborhoods and buildings. We have been in a buyer's market for the past two years, so I don't expect prices to go much lower. Since August, buyers have come back because mortgage rates and prices are both at historical lows. Every neighborhood is a little different; however, nowhere is there a fire sale happening.

Now I see buyers thinking about how they want to live their life in their apartments. Before the pandemic, you could easily escape to the city itself. Now, people think, oh, I might be here for six weeks straight, how do I want to live in my space? The priorities have shifted a bit. Many people seek out areas with more parks to be out and about instead of dense areas. Having a separate workspace has become a top priority. It's really about what is important to them, and that might just be having a glass of wine on the balcony.

What do showings look like in the epicenter of the pandemic? Are you doing more virtual or in-person?

Melissa Vance: We're doing showings in person. However, you see more video and Matterport (3-D Virtual) than you did pre-pandemic. For some clients, I have done Zoom/FaceTime tours for them as well. All showings are by appointment since we don't have open houses anymore. We take stopping the virus's spread very seriously, so some forms have been implemented. These forms need to be signed confirming you don't have a temperature over 98.6 degrees Fahrenheit or 37 degrees Celsius, have not tested positive for COVID-19, or have not been in contact with anyone who has tested positive for COVID-19. We have to inquire about travel and vacations since about 35 states require quarantine when returning to New York State. And, of course, masks are mandatory for inside buildings. All of this has become our new normal.

What inspired you to get started in real estate?

Melissa Vance: My family has been in real estate in Upper Manhattan for the past 100 years. A few years ago, I inherited my share of two buildings. I decided to get my real estate license to understand the asset. I just fell in love with the whole industry and process. I deal with many different sellers, buyers, and investors. Whether it be first-time homebuyers, investment properties, buying for children, pied-à-terre, multi-family, new development, or 1031 Exchanges. I also deal with many rentals and advise other property owners. The variety of things I do keeps it exciting, fun, and engaging.

How can buyers and sellers in the Manhattan area find you and connect with you?

Melissa Vance: I can always be reached on my cell at 917-703-6378 or email at melissa.vance@sothebyshomes.com. And, you can search Manhattan and Brooklyn listings on my website: www.melissavancenyc.com.

MELISSA VANCE

Associate Real Estate Broker, Sotheby's International Realty NY

Melissa is a successful associate broker, highly accomplished at the art of providing exceptional service and top-notch marketing. Whether working with buyers, sellers, or investors of residential real estate, she makes a personal commitment with everyone she works with. Her acute analytical skills have been invaluable in guiding and advising her clients with regard to the pricing and marketing of their properties. She is devoted to not only exceeding her clients' goals but also ensuring accurate information and expert knowledge, so her clients always feel positive and satisfied with their decisions. Melissa's clients rely on her strong negotiation skills, knowledge, diligence, and creativity. Her desire to provide superior service to her clientele is balanced by her approachable personality.

Melissa's family has been part of New York real estate for the past 100 years. She provides a unique perspective on NY properties. Before becoming an associate broker, Melissa was an advertising executive working with Fortune 500 clients to develop their global strategies. She is able to leverage her global marketing experience and real estate acumen to develop tailored and effective marketing campaigns for her clients.

Melissa is devoted to maintaining long-lasting relationships built on mutual respect with all of her clients. Her hobbies and passions include golfing, skiing, traveling, cooking, wine tasting, nutrition, and exercise.

WEBSITE:

www.melissavancenyc.com

EMAIL:

melissa.vance@sothebyshomes.com

LINKEDIN:

linkedin.com/in/melissavance/

FACEBOOK PROFILE:

facebook.com/melissa.vance2

AMERICA'S LEADING REAL ESTATE PROFESSIONALS

FACEBOOK PAGE:
facebook.com/melissavancenyc

TWITTER:
twitter.com/MelVance

INSTAGRAM:
instagram.com/melissa_vance_nyc/

OFFICE:
212.606.7630

CELL:
917.703.6378

ADDRESS:
650 Madison Avenue | New York, NY 10022

Conversation with Erin Newman

Tell us about your business and the people you specialize in helping.

Erin Newman: I have enjoyed this business. Having raised a very large family, I bought and sold homes before I was an agent; investment properties were also a part of my portfolio. When I got into this business, I realized I could make such a difference with just a connection with people. I thrive on building relationships, figuring out what is best for the client, and getting them to whatever results they desire. I've handled everything from low end $90,000 condos to over $1 million properties. It just depends on who needs the service and how I can best help. I have a tremendous comfortableness working in the Phoenix Metro area as I was born and raised in the Scottsdale area. Living here most of my life and raising my six children here has been a tremendous asset to my business.

How has the pandemic affected real estate in the greater Phoenix area, and what is the market like currently?

Erin Newman: Today, our market is definitely a seller's market. We have people flooding into our area anywhere from 200-250 people per day. Therefore, we have limited housing. And so for a buyer, the market is very competitive. For a seller, fix it up, list it at a fair price, and you'll do just fine. As far as the pandemic, when it first hit, I had many things in escrow. And it was kind of like, what do you do? As always, I just kept moving forward. Some people are leerier of the germs and people in their homes than others. So it just depends on what that person needs as far as working around the issues of today.

I had a transaction recently where everything was done via video, and then at the last minute, the client decided to come into the actual home and take a look. I have been doing virtual showings and remote buying for years; I previously was involved with international sales where people were always buying homes sight unseen. It just requires a lot of communication and video. For the people who choose to see houses in person, we just pop on a mask and do our best not to touch things inside the home.

Are there things buyers and sellers need to consider today that are different than in the past?

Erin Newman: As far as the buyers, today's unique situation is that prices are rapidly increasing. During the pandemic, I had clients I was working with who got COVID, pulled back from the purchase, stayed home, and the price point of the home jumped during that short amount of time. Now they are just on hold since prices are increasing leaps and bounds. Buyers need to be serious and stick with it. Rates are still relatively low, but there is limited inventory.

For sellers, I prioritize developing a game plan because I don't want my clients to sell and then not be able to find what they are looking for. So there are a lot of moving pieces. Sellers should know their goals, where they are going, and then we can work from there. I think it's better to be out of the house right now due to the pandemic's health concerns, but each client has a unique situation.

What inspired you to get started in real estate?

Erin Newman: I was married for 30 years, raised six children, and then went through a divorce. I then went through my infamous, "What do I want to be when I grow up?" at 50 years old. I researched many options. My background is in Science. I was Pre-Med but didn't go that route since I started a family. I decided on real estate because home is so important. Especially during this pandemic, we realize the value of the home. Helping clients find the right home and seeing the happiness it brings them is very satisfying. At Thanksgiving and Christmas, my clients invite me over as one of their family; I am always invited to birthday parties and baptisms. It is a great feeling to help people in that capacity.

How can people that could benefit from your expertise find you and connect with you?

Erin Newman: I'm Erin Newman with Erin Newman Fine Homes.

My phone number is 480-466-8193. My website is ErinNewmanFineHomes.com. I can be reached via email at ErinNewmanAZ@gmail.com.

ERIN NEWMAN

Broker-Owner
Erin Newman Fine Homes

Erin Newman, CEO and founder of Erin Newman Fine Homes, is a Scottsdale, Arizona native through and through. Her deep relationships with family and friends have allowed Erin Newman Fine Homes to become a "house sold" name in the Valley of the Sun. The oldest of two growing up in Scottsdale, Arizona, Erin learned the value of community and the importance of the home from a young age. High school accomplishments included being the Saguaro Sabercat; this was a short-lived gig as there was no air conditioning in her day's mascot suits. She decided that it was too hot to entertain the stands with record heat over 100 degrees.

Erin spent a considerable part of her married life raising six children. She grew up in the flooring industry as a child. She started Premiere Wood Floors with her husband; the company was a leader in the custom wood flooring industry. Her strength in business, combined with her precision in detailed tasks, was a natural transition into real estate. She negotiated through an involved divorce, which enhanced her current real estate negotiating skills. With a 30-year resume of sales performance awards, team leadership positions, and business development experience – Erin combines her love for real estate with her caring skills that have helped her become a real estate industry-leading Broker.

Erin's successful family and her knowledge of dealing with clients have enabled her to understand any successful real estate agent's single most important trait: what people want. One of Erin's best attributes is her ability to be discreet about her client's private information; this is important to Erin as she deals with clients that do not want their personal information to be discussed with others. Erin commits daily to finding the perfect home for buyers; she also successfully sells homes minimizing the stress that may occur. Erin's passion for excellence is exhibited by the clients that treat her like family.

Would you like to know more information about Erin? She was voted "Class Clown" at Saguaro High in 1981; she did stand up comedy in the Bay Area in the late 1980s. If you want to work with someone knowledgeable and FUN, then Erin is your one!

WEBSITE:

ErinNewmanFineHomes.com

EMAIL:

ErinNewmanAZ@gmail.com

PHONE:

480-466-8193

FACEBOOK:

https://www.facebook.com/erinmiminewman/

LINKEDIN:

https://www.linkedin.com/in/erinnewmanrealestate/

Conversation with Tammy Potter

Tell us about your business and the people you specialize in helping.

Tammy Potter: I am both a Buyer and Seller's Realtor, whether it's homes, land, or commercial property. My job is to understand and navigate each part of the transaction and problem solve, if necessary, to face any bumps along the way. Sometimes it's like putting together a puzzle; you want to make sure you have all the pieces perfectly fit in the right place.

It's my job to see my client's perfect picture and have it picture-perfect at the end.

I feel communication and education help each of my clients better understand each phase of a real estate transaction. Having a clear understanding of credit scores, down payments, lender's responsibilities, escrow and title information, and all the phrases and terms which may be new to them explained and clarified is one of my favorite parts of being a Realtor.

As a Realtor, helping my clients accomplish their real estate dreams is my reward.

How has the current pandemic affected the San Diego real estate market?

Tammy Potter: When the pandemic first hit, I honestly thought my career would be dead in the water. Then my phone started ringing, and I completed five transactions in a row. The minute I had one sale in escrow, I was onto the next deal, helping the next client into the next house. The one thing 2020 has done for Real Estate is to help renters turn into homeowners and help sellers upgrade into that next home or move out of state. Low-interest rates help real estate tremendously. For example, I have one particular client who has been waiting to buy a home. He was able to buy a four-bedroom house and rent out part of it to help pay the mortgage. With a current interest rate of 3%, this low rate is fantastic for sellers because inventory is low, and with so many more people who have new opportunities to buy, it's created quick turn-around time. One house I sold was on the market for only three days. I listed the house on Thursday at 10:00 pm, and I had showings on Friday/Saturday. I had multiple qualified loan approved offers from buyers. The sellers were able to pick a buyer by Sunday, and we were in escrow by Monday morning. This is the time for people to make positive changes in their lives.

Have you seen people's priorities change during these times? What concerns do you hear from clients now that are different from pre-pandemic problems?

Tammy Potter: Before the pandemic, the usual concerns were, "If we sell our house, are we going to be able to get into the house we want?" Buyers who want to buy a home in a particular school district with low inventory worry about the possibility of multiple offers on a home. Those are still concerns, but what has changed due to the pandemic is that many rental properties want to sell, and they cannot evict their current tenants. We are seeing many "cash for keys," which means renters are being paid an incentive plus their deposits to move out of a residence. The real estate market is thriving due to this low-interest rate, and that motivation is a driving force even during a pandemic. Some people have options and opportunities they didn't have before the pandemic hit.

What is the number one piece of advice you are giving out to buyers and sellers in today's market?

Tammy Potter: Talk with your local realtor or lender about the market. Ensure that you have the money to cover the cost of buying or selling a home. Without a pre-approved loan, you are not in the market. We have turned into a market of "be ready" buyers. There's no more "looky-loos" or thinking, "I might want to buy this house." Your paperwork has to be done, and you have to be ready to make an offer. So if you're looking to buy, get pre-approved....then call me!

How did you get started in real estate, and what inspired you?

Tammy Potter: When I was 19 years old, my aunt became a real estate agent. My aunt was a big influence in my life. I worked for Century 21 & Escrow in Tierrasanta. I would do open houses, stuff mailers, call clients and work in the escrow department. My aunt said to me, "Get your money to work for you instead of you working for your money." My father followed that same advice and our family has built our financial foundation on real estate.

Growing up here in San Diego, I've seen the many changes in real estate and the real estate market. But I have always had my heart and my head in agreement that San Diego real estate is one of the best you could ever invest in. We have a consistent market that offers buyers and sellers investment properties to rent, beautiful homes near the ocean to live in, stunning hills, or our thriving downtown, whether it be new or historic.

In general I simply love real estate. It's a puzzle to me. The beginning and ending are the same. You have all the same pieces for the real estate transaction. It's how the transaction falls together that is different every time. Coordinating that whole thing is very appealing to me. I love helping people fulfill their dreams of buying a house. There is nothing better than handing the keys over to brand new homeowners. This is what I love to do.

For people who could benefit from your expertise and help, how can they find you and connect with you?

Tammy Potter: My website is AskStammy.com. I use all forms of communication. Call Me, Text Me or Email Me. Tammypotter14@gmail.com or 858-213-1963. Can Zoom too.

TAMMY POTTER

Realtor
eXp Realty of California, Inc.

Throughout my life, I've always been able to combine what I love, helping people, cooking, and real estate in my careers. I feel when you can use your natural talents in your career, you enjoy what you do.

I've owned a small cafe serving up lunch specials, afternoon pastries, and coffee. I loved baking and planning my menus and serving my customers. I always wanted them to feel they were in my kitchen.

I always said my last career would be in Real Estate. In 2014, I got my license. It has been exciting ever since. When I can help people understand the maze of homeownership or selling their home, it's truly a life reward to me.

WEBSITE:

AskStammy.com

EMAIL:

Tammypotter14@gmail.com

LINKEDIN:

https://www.linkedin.com/in/tammy-potter-56915731/

FACEBOOK:

https://www.facebook.com/tammy.pottermarden/

CELL:

858-257-2202

ABOUT THE PUBLISHER

Mark Imperial is a Best-Selling Author, Syndicated Business Columnist, Syndicated Radio Host, and internationally recognized Stage, Screen, and Radio Host of numerous business shows spotlighting leading experts, entrepreneurs, and business celebrities.

His passion is to discover noteworthy business owners, professionals, experts, and leaders who do great work and share their stories and secrets to their success with the world on his syndicated radio program titled "Remarkable Radio."

Mark is also the media marketing strategist and voice for some of the world's most famous brands. You can hear his voice over the airwaves weekly on Chicago radio and worldwide on iHeart Radio.

Mark is a Karate black belt, teaches kickboxing, loves Thai food, House Music, and his favorite TV shows are infomercials.

Learn more:

www.MarkImperial.com

www.ImperialAction.com

www.RemarkableRadioShow.com

www.ingramcontent.com/pod-product-compliance
Lightning Source LLC
Chambersburg PA
CBHW071110210326
41519CB00020B/6251